SOME OF MY FAVOURITE THINGS

Edited by

Sarah Marshall

First published in Great Britain in 2004 by
POETRY NOW
Remus House,
Coltsfoot Drive,
Peterborough, PE2 9JX
Telephone (01733) 898101
Fax (01733) 313524

SB ISBN 1 84460 826 3

FOREWORD

Although we are a nation of poets we are accused of not reading poetry, or buying poetry books. After many years of listening to the incessant gripes of poetry publishers, I can only assume that the books they publish, in general, are books that most people do not want to read.

Poetry should not be obscure, introverted, and as cryptic as a crossword puzzle: it is the poet's duty to reach out and embrace the world.

The world owes the poet nothing and we should not be expected to dig and delve into a rambling discourse searching for some inner meaning.

The reason we write poetry (and almost all of us do) is because we want to communicate: an ideal; an idea; or a specific feeling. Poetry is as essential in communication, as a letter; a radio; a telephone, and the main criterion for selecting the poems in this anthology is very simple: they communicate.

CONTENTS

The Journey (Part Two)	Sheila Atkinson	1
Instinctive Ways	Margaret Ann Wheatley	2
Mother	Nancy Elliott	3
Memories Of Childhood	Diana Daley	4
School Holidays	Kinsman Clive	5
Memories	Peter Chaney	6
Reflection	Patrick Ayton	7
Maybe One Day	Pauline E Reynolds	8
Why I Am What I Am	Allen Jessop	9
Our Dream Cottage . . .	E J A Healey - The Warrior Poet	10
When I Close My Eyes	Donald John Tye	12
Musical Magic	S J Dodwell	13
My Home	Ada E Redhead	14
Rugby Passion	Carol Hanney	16
Labour Of Love	Robin Morgan	17
Acceptance	Jo Lee	18
The Sound Of Relaxation	Liz Kerry	19
The Laughing Cavalier	John Paulley	20
The Best Things In Life	Violetta Jean Ferguson	21
Saturday Shop	J Bailey	22
The Antique World	Hardeep Singh-Leader	23
My Friends	J L Thomas	24
Swimming Pool	Mike Tracey	25
My Little Fluffy Bunny	Irene Morris	26
The Best Things In Life	Beryl Mitchell	27
Contentment	Annie Morrice	28
For The Best	G Knapton	29
Little White Pet	Jacqui Beddow	30
Time	M Wilcox	31
The Learning Journey	Marjorie Picton	32
Best Things In Life	Sylvia Kellett	33
Who Knows How Long!	Richard Ninnis	34
The Best Things In Life	Janet Cavill	35
The Best Things In Life	Dot Ridings	36
The Hush Of Evening	John Clarke	37
Best Things In Life	Candida Lovell-Smith	38

Seasons Of Life	Val Bermingham	39
Gems For Free	Anita Richards	40
Discovery	Peter Davies	41
For All But The Best Is Within	Mark Anthony Noble	42
A Picture	Gary J Finlay	43
Best Things In Life	Richard Morris	44
Rock-A-Bye Boating	Pearl M Burdock	45
High Days And Holidays	M C Jones	46
Precious Daughters	Barbara Harrison	47
Songs We Sang	Brian Conway	48
The Soul's Persistent Whisper	Anthony Fagg	49
Bluebells	Jean Wallington	50
The Bestest In All The World	Elaine Priscilla Kilshaw	51
Little Wiggles	Belinda Summerfield	52
Heaven And Hell	E M Doyle	53
Caravan Days	Celia Auld	54
Dreaming	Barbara Brown	55
Grandad	George Carrick	56
True Love	Sheila Waller	57
A Daughter's Thank You	Samantha Connolly	58
Our Mum And Nan	Sandra Jebb	59
God's Little Angel	A Navamani	60
To My Wonderful Gran ... With Love	Louise Pamela Webster	61
Our Daughter	Peter R Salter	62
Grub Up	Brian O'Brien	63
Branching Out	Josephine Anne Dunworth	64
My Wife, My Life	Philip Peartree	65
My Father	Ann Margaret Rowell	66
Luna	Desmond Swords	67
Thank You	M Smith	68
Someone I Never Knew	Susan Fear	69
With You	Tiffany Little	70
Aunt Edith's Birthday Treat	J Dalton Taylor	71
Together We ...	Gerald Weeks	72
Sisters	Lorraine Booth	73
5 Years Ago	Nikki Rogers	74
Precious Moments	David Wright	75

Farewell	Martin Blakemore Davis	76
Torn	Melanie May	78
The Mirror	Kay Hancock	80
A Bear And Two Mints	AnnMarie Eldon	82
My Family	Sylvia J Barbier	83
Fiery Influence!	George Penev	84
Joan	Dot Brown	86
Advice To A Son	William Archibald	87
Just Say No	Tim Thompson	88
Memories	Hilda Morrall	89
To Rita	Shirley Ann Bunyan	90
To My Friend	Peter Holmes	92

THE JOURNEY (PART TWO)

From psychological silence to deafening mental screams
A sinister spectre creeps into our dreams.

Flashbacks from the past of villagers' violence
Evil monochrome memories where there should be silence.

Through our children's eyes we again will see
The beauty of a snowflake, our minds now set free.

Like children we are travelling, helping each other along
Learning to live and love, beginning to belong.

Time to let go of the pain of the past
Not quite journey's end but some peace at last.

Not enough violence that's what the cops said
Against the evil uncle who wished my brother dead.

Trying to cover their guilt, my mother and her brothers
Living the high life, but what about the others.

We live with the pain, abandoned once more
No bridges left to build, we close another door.

Looking to the future we wait for a tomorrow
Where there's peace of mind and there's no more sorrow.

Not going down that road, that's what they all said
No feelings of loss, in my eyes they're dead.

Sheila Atkinson

INSTINCTIVE WAYS

A baby's smile,
those perfectly formed fingers and toes
- creation so blessed.

An artist's touch,
such deftly worked talent and skill
- expressions all shared.

With music's gifts,
love succinctly breathes emotion and sound
- enriching each moment.

Margaret Ann Wheatley

MOTHER

M is for the million things you do.
O is for one no better.
T is for the tears you shed for me.
H is for the happiness you bring to all.
E is for the everlasting love you give.
R is to remind us of the care your loving heart bestowed on us
                                   when we were young.

Nancy Elliott

MEMORIES OF CHILDHOOD

As I was sitting alone in the park
I found my mind wandering into the past
Recalling favourite places and happy times
Paddling in the river Nene at Stanground
And trying to learn how to swim
Not succeeding but having fun
One winter skating and sliding on the ice
When the fields had flooded over from the river
Taking a jam jar and catching tiddlers
Or chasing butterflies with a net
The river branched off from the Nene at Peterborough
And we often walked across the fields into the city
Learning to ride a bicycle on the road outside
Mona let go of the seat and I was on my own
Going downhill with a bend at the bottom
Not knowing how to steer or stop, I just jumped off
But soon I had mastered the art of cycling
Then playing hopscotch, skipping and hide and seek
Flying home-made kites in the sky
Then going home to Mum's Victoria plum jam and crusty bread
Oh, happy, happy days at Stanground
But all too soon they were at an end
For we moved when I was eleven
And with homework and household chores to do
For me childhood was over.

Diana Daley

SCHOOL HOLIDAY

The grandchildren *have come to stay!*
The guest room is in disarray.
'Grandpa! We *must* have somewhere to play!'
In *their* toilet, things seem a little rum.
The seat is stuck down with chewing gum!
The toilet roll is much reduced in size.
What remains lies in folds upon the floor.
Was a cream puppy seen near the door?

My granddaughter is on the kitchen steps,
reaching up to the cupboard which I *had*
designated *out of reach of children!*
'Grandpa . . .
why have you moved that huge biscuit tin
where you keep all your lovely chocolate?

Grandpa?'
'Well?'
'May we come again? Soon?'
'Well . . . yes . . .
yes, of course you may.
Now. Don't forget your pocket money . . .
and . . . chocolate.
Be sure to give your chewing gum
to your lovely mum!'

Now they are gone, I can relax
and swear as much - as - I like!

Kinsman Clive

MEMORIES

The past remembered,
Good old days, bad old days,
In silence retrospect,
They reach out to us,
With untouchable feeling,
Memories,
Those elapsed fragments of time,
Sombre, light, they summon us,
They arrest our minds,
How can we touch them,
How can we retain them,
Other than in thought?

Peter Chaney

REFLECTION

Regret is the only thought that dominates my mind
Searching for the truth: which answers do I want to believe?
That I'm a victim and that I would never purposely deceive
But caught up in circumstances and situations that I never
                                        should have been in
It's hard to believe there is an end before there is a beginning

Every kind word, every loving embrace brings me back to
                when you found out and that look of hurt on your face
You don't return my calls; you walk away when you see me,
What hope do I have if you don't even speak to me?
I have a calm exterior but inside I'm screaming
It's hard to believe there is an end before there is a beginning

It's an everyday occurrence between males and females;
Sending love letters and e-mails, going for long walks on sand
                                        and seashells
Always take the chance but you never can tell because not
                        all that starts well ends well
I haven't seen you in a while and it got me thinking
It's hard to believe there is an end before there is a beginning

Patrick Ayton

MAYBE ONE DAY

I dream of a world
where people can walk, without fear.

I dream of a world
where children can play, and feel safe.

I dream of a world
where a smile is real, and not the fact that
deep inside, you really want to cry.

I dream of a world
where there is no war, no bombs, no guns.

I dream of a world
where there is no struggle or pain.

I dream of a world
where there is no hatred, only love.

I dream of a world
where there is no suffering,
everyone is happy and free,
and we all unite, and live in
perfect harmony.

Who knows,
maybe one day.

Pauline E Reynolds

WHY I AM WHAT I AM

My childhood was spent in a period of economic gloom
When every event appeared to threaten a penurious doom.
Yet my memories of those days are not of sorrow and regret
For to those straitened times I owe a sense of debt.

The values I absorbed were to benefit me when mature;
I learned to appreciate life in simple terms for the future.
I needed not the accoutrements of wealth
As, for me, to be rich was to be sound in health.

My sisters and brothers learned to appreciate our pleasures,
Often by merely sharing our limited treasures;
A comic paper divided, a page to each of us,
Each week an event we regarded so truly joyous.

A walk on Sunday together to the local park
Often sealed the week of work as a high mark.
More exciting were the days of picking blackberries
With Dad leading his band of fruit mercenaries.

Discipline was firm but not oppressive in form
With Dad's word the last one usually the norm.
Mum controlled daily events with a firm hand
Which occasionally was literally used if we failed to understand.

My first decade ended as our family was affected by war;
Evacuation took us away from all we knew before
And it was some time before reunion saw us together again.
But things were never quite the same; the pattern had been broken.

The next few years led me through adolescence as I met each stage;
High school, exams, jobs as a paper boy, Man City; a living wage,
All developments seeming to have been inevitable advances
Which have sown the seeds of my current circumstances.

Allen Jessop

OUR DREAM COTTAGE . . .

The leaves are on the edge of life as the winds of autumn skip along
And now all the sweet, fast-flowing crystal streams join the wind
in its song
I watched a toad in fleeting chase leaping high over dirt
and chiselled stones
And in the distance I heard a foaming splash as the toad dived in
with icy moans
Yet where on the grassy, mossy bank I stand, I am indeed
with love beguiled
As autumn rain begins falling - falling slowly down, I am glad
it's only mild.

I live in a dream cottage down a quiet country lane, people stop
and take a peep
Into my garden and my cottage's name, it's called 'The Love Nest',
with love I keep
There's an old wrought iron gate fixed to a wall and a
green picket fence so neat
And in my garden there're lots of flowers, foxgloves, purple,
pink and blue, smelling sweet
There's crazy paving from the gate to the door where a
single stone gnome sits
Sweet honeysuckle fills the air with fragrance as birds flock, robins,
sparrow and tits.

In one corner there's a tiny little rowan tree with bright shining
orange berries
Where a blackbird warbles with delight and eating all the berries
like cherries
There's two nesting boxes, one high up in an apple tree, the other
fixed to a wall
And in the one in the apple tree is the blackbird's family, I can hear
her fledglings call
The other on our cottage wall, in it a red-breasted song-tuned
robin alone sits
Awaiting the new birth of her young while her mate is collecting
for the nest bits.

Our dream cottage with flowers all growing up and strong as
autumn slips in
My wife and I in Cutteslowe, the northern part of Oxford, are living,
we sweetly spin
Our dream cottage is a bungalow down in Templar Road,
there're roses up around our door
Cascading down around our windowpanes, smelling oh so sweet,
who could ask for more?
Just across the road there's a village shop selling packets and boxes,
candles and ice cream
Biscuits, sausages, jam, paraffin, cheese, bacon, chicken and
lots of cans of beans.

E J A Healy - The Warrior Poet

WHEN I CLOSE MY EYES

Every night when I close my eyes
I dream of the times, Marie
Of the very happy times
You and I walked hand in hand
Through the golden flower-
Filled woodland
And ran side by side
Along the golden sands
Under a bright silver moonlit night

But we are now old and grey
And by my side you have always stayed
And you still look as beautiful, Marie
As you did when I first met you
On that golden sunlit day
Nearly forty-five years ago now

You still look like an angel
From up in Heaven above
An angel of beauty I will always love
With the whole of my heart and soul
Your angel-blue eyes still sparkle
Brighter than the stars above
And you still make me feel
Like a millionaire
Every time I hold you close to my heart
And thank the good Lord above
For an angel of beauty like you, Marie
In my very, very lucky life

Donald John Tye

MUSICAL MAGIC

The other day
I was carried away
By music so strong,
It could scarcely belong
To the world around
As I heard the sound
Of four inspired musicians
Seated in various positions
Playing with such feeling
It left one reeling
That notes could
From a piece of wood
Emit such power
That fills the hour
With astonishment
For sounds, Heaven-sent
To ravish the ear
To banish fear
To lift one above
To a world of love
To heights unknown
To some celestial throne
To joy and elation
All from music and its creation!

S J Dodwell

MY HOME

Alone in the twilight, the fires burnt low
My thoughts wander back to days long ago
A small country cottage with windowpanes small
The jasmine that grew on the front garden wall

The apple and plum trees and flowers so gay
The old wooden hut where I used to play
Inside the cottage the fire burnt bright
In an old-fashioned grate, the hearthstone snow-white

The fender was steel, but like silver it shone
With a poker, a shovel and tongs resting on
The home-made cloth rugs covered the floor
And a home-made green toy cupboard near the back door

Some beautiful thoughts in my memory remain
As I picture the clock with its brass weights and chains
The hands slowly moved round its big round face
Day and night it tick-tocked at the same old pace

Sometimes I picture, I see once more
The red roses in bloom around the front door
The scent of the honeysuckle in the cool evening breeze
Not forgetting the beauty of everlasting sweet peas

Still my thoughts wander back, and plainly I see
The cottage inside, as it once used to be
Everything cosy, clean and neat
A table well spread, with plenty to eat

Brothers and sisters, happy at play
Mother and Dad kept busy all day
Washing and mending, gardening too
Whatever the problem they always pulled through

From dawn of the day till dark comes the night
These pictures to me will always be bright
As I pause for a while, more beauty I see
On faces I love, still smiling at me

Ada E Redhead

RUGBY PASSION

The oval ball kicked high in the sky
It's been known to make grown men cry
Catch him fast before he has a chance to make that pass
Now it's the scrum
Pushing and pulling
Grinding and thumping
Sets our hearts faster pumping
We hold our breath as a try is made
Yes! Yes! He has it done
Boy oh boy, we're having such fun
I look around at all the fans
Jumping around and clapping their hands
The highs and the lows
We love it all
What would we do for that oval ball
Kicked high in the sky
Then you can see grown men cry
Their passion and pride they cannot hide

Carol Hanney

LABOUR OF LOVE

My favourite pastime is ironing, getting
the clothes looking nice with no creases
in them, and then neatly folding into
piles to be put away in cupboards and
drawers so when we go out our clothes look
nice on us.
Ironing is a nice hobby which people should
take their time over and not try to rush
so take your time over your ironing and I am
sure you will enjoy it as much as I do.

Robin Morgan

ACCEPTANCE

Oh to climb an apple tree
In leafy shade around me see
the fragrant fruit, and stay
up there a little while
to sweetly pass the time away . . .

Oh to conquer a mountain high
There to fly
a pennant in the snow upon its peak
and in the cold pure air
redemption seek . . .

Oh to climb the tallest spire
Watch the world in
miniature below, while I
contemplate a little there
somewhere between the Earth and sky . . .

Now climbing days are over
I walk on solid ground
And on the daily round
pray for grace
to seek my joys within the
limits of the given space . . .
To find apples fallen in the
wind and rain
Breathe mountain air from lower plain
and take my view on life
Not from the sky
but from down on Earth to
up on high
And thank God for the enabling so to do.

Jo Lee

THE SOUND OF RELAXATION

I cannot live without it,
However hard I try,
I often see it sitting there,
Always catching my eye,

It's hard to relax without it,
Silently calling my name,
Willing me to touch it,
To join in with its game,

Sitting right in front of it,
Trying to decide,
Which one I'm in the mood for,
As they all sit side by side,

Then suddenly it happens,
My hands have done the deed,
I take one from the pile,
I know which one I need,

My head is loudly banging,
With the sound of Slayer,
Oh how I love,
My CD player!

Liz Kerry

THE LAUGHING CAVALIER

The smiling face upon the wall,
It hung for years in oak-walled hall;
For countless students, faces alight,
It truly was an inspiring sight.

Through days of tests the picture hung,
It never changed when hymns were sung;
The smiling face a source of power,
A mammoth help in crucial hours.

The school so new with hall so great,
A shining beacon in war-torn state;
When nearby bombs caused damage and mess,
The picture safe, all sound, no stress.

For countless years the smile in place,
Throughout the war, through years of grace;
For art and history our picture a boon,
The guilded frame just shone like the moon.

The day now came for closing the door,
The handsome hall would be no more;
For Foster's School the end in sight,
For Cavalier 'twas time for fight.

'Twas sad to see the famous site,
With piles of rubble to massive height;
Our thanks to Mike, the smile still beams,
For Cavalier life full of dreams.

The Cavalier is on my wall,
The memories I can well recall;
Of truth and trust and faith so great,
Of teachers who were all first rate.

John Paulley

THE BEST THINGS IN LIFE

A little wave to cheer me on
A goodnight kiss when day is done
A gentle hug, a warm embrace
A comforting word and a smiling face.

An arm to lean on when growing old
A nice warm fire when days are cold
The sun's appearance after a storm
The cry of a baby, newly born.

The friend who will take you by the hand
And tell you that they understand
Perhaps when you are feeling low
They tell you that you're nice to know.

The smell of a flower that grows in spring
The sound of church bells when they ring
The best things in life are always free
For everyone, including you and me.

Violetta Jean Ferguson

SATURDAY SHOP

Shopping on a Saturday,
Crooked spire in view,
The sun is shining, bells are ringing,
I feel happy, not blue.

Crowds of busy people,
All hurrying by,
Lots of different colours,
Like a rainbow in the sky.

Pass by the church,
Lovely bride and groom,
Bridesmaids amidst the confetti,
It's over all too soon.

Different kinds of music,
Are playing every week,
It's all part of the Saturday shop,
Life, fun, there in the street.

J Bailey

THE ANTIQUE WORLD

Bullet shells and medals,
I feel like a peddler on pedals,
About forty old pennies,
1873, mind-boggling, phewee!
St George so blue, I clean the spores
As stamping was galore!
'Twas the letters through the war,
Accumulating on a surplus store,
Driving medals 1965,
That's my DOB, cor!
It was currency that swept so,
Impure, that's what I endure!
Stamp collectors really mature,
Whilst I once did the apex,
Of snails right down to the aperture.
Three pence and a half a penny
Could I have bought a spinning Jenny?
And what I perchance an emerald
Just as luck ran it, it ran out.
As a given away collectable

Hardeep Singh-Leader

MY FRIENDS

There's so many things that make me cry,
And even more that make me smile,
But without a friend to share them with,
None of it would be worthwhile.

I love to sit when I'm alone,
And write a line or two,
But how sad would it be if when I'm done,
I had no one to show it to?

I love to watch my daughter grow,
She learns something new every day,
But I couldn't imagine not telling my mates,
What new things she can say.

I like to set myself new goals,
To keep me in the game,
But how many would I actually reach
Without my friends to keep me sane?

I love to do so many things,
Just not alone because I love to be,
With my friends who make my life complete,
They're the ones who make me . . . me.

J L Thomas

SWIMMING POOL

Smell of chlorine in my nose, at the swimming pool I arrive
At the pool edge enter the water with a standard dive
For a split second in the air, noise is all around
Splash, I hit the water, now it's just a muffled sound

Like being in space, weightless, I stretch my body out
But the surface beckons me to return to the noise and shouts
Up, up I go, reaching shattering chaos once again
Start dodging people to reach the swimming lane

Check goggles are fitting snugly on my head
Don't want the chlorine to make my eyes all red
Push off from the side to commence my first length
Starting off gently so as to build up all my strength

Legs kicking, arms spreading, I start to swim
Blowing out under water, on the surface breathing in
Occasionally get it wrong so a horrid price I pay
Warm swimming pool water tastes nasty, this I have to say

Adrenaline flowing, heart pumping, feels real good inside
Exhilaration flows over me like an ebb tide
Not counting lengths, just swimming, swimming on full power
For soon it's warm down time, then leg it for a shower

Mike Tracey

MY LITTLE FLUFFY BUNNY

On my way to school each day
For a while I liked to stay
And sitting on a gate, into a field I look
At the animals grazing near the brook

Today I saw a rabbit small
Running amongst the grass so tall
His coat was soft and fluffy
His eyes all pink and puffy

He was playing about so happily
That I don't think he even noticed me
His antics really were very funny
And I decided to call him Fluffy Bunny

I would love to take you home with me
But I know that can never be
Instead I will bring you back a treat
Like a nice juicy carrot for you to eat

Please don't be afraid of me
As I want to be your friend you see
For a moment he sat up and looked around
Listening for any strange noise or sound

Then afraid of predators and of man
Back into his burrow he quickly ran
So bye for now my fluffy bunny, see you soon
It may even be tomorrow afternoon

Irene Morris

THE BEST THINGS IN LIFE

There really is no contest
For the best things in my life
It was when you proposed to me
Asking me to be your wife.

We found ourselves a place to live
In the countryside we chose
With a perfect cottage garden
Room for vegetable and rose.

We took our vows in April
I was as happy as could be
Surrounded by our family and friends
We honeymooned in Tenby.

We settled into married life
Just one thing to complete
Our family needed additions
With the patter of tiny feet.

The autumn days of '74
When leaves began to fall
Brought joy and happiness
To our lives, our loving son, Paul.

Our cottage in the country
We began to fill and share
In the springtime of '78
With the arrival of daughter Clare.

I daily count my blessings
For the best things in my life
Are you, husband, son and daughter
From a mother and a wife.

Beryl Mitchell

CONTENTMENT

The fire crackles in the grate and warms my tired face
and all the riches of the world are landed in this place.
Sorrow's hold can take no more my heart and troubled mind,
tonight it cannot grip me, as I contentment find
and if I could capture moments and take them to my heart,
I'd share them out amongst the world where they could joy impart.

Annie Morrice

FOR THE BEST

In my eyes it can't be beaten
That little pill
So often sweetens
Give it to the meek
A toke for the weak

Opium in masses
Dipped in a little molasses
Pharmacy's gift for the working classes

A token to conformity
Governed placation
Can't see
Suppressed nation

It's so sweet
Your problems they handle
Mould you like wax into candle

Don't worry though
A medical gift
Saccharin-coated wonder
Your spirits to lift

Smile and drift along
Once weak, now strong

Don't ever begin to question
They'll take your sweeties
So, learn their lesson

Ignorant devotion
The only rule
Keep it up
Really . . .
It's for the best

G Knapton

LITTLE WHITE PET

White and fluffy, noisy but sweet
Barking at anyone out in the street
Looking, watching and running around
Digging up bulbs we've put in the ground.

Playing with snails, or biting your toe
Her antics keep us all on the go
Shows off for a while then gambols instead
And promptly flakes out in her bed.

She's loving and bright, with pointed ears
Coal-black eyes and no known fears
She looks for a trophy to steal and hide
Likes to play chase in the garden outside.

She knows the car's sound, excitedly barking
Knowing her daddy's only just parking
He'll soon be in to give her a fuss and a cuddle
Running around him, getting all in a muddle.

She's trusting and loving, cute as can be
When she's all clean, she's white and lovely
Dirty and flirty, with a lovely face
Dashing about all over the place.

She sleeps on the bed
Likes cuddling her ted
Growls if you move just a mite
She's a loveable, adorable tyke.

Jacqui Beddow

TIME

The most precious thing for me, is time,
I never have enough,
I'd like to turn the clock off,
So I could do *my* stuff.

The pace of life is much too fast,
No time to cry, and less to laugh,
We charge around from A to B,
But where's the time for you and me,
To stop, take stock, enjoy the day?
There really seems no other way,
To earn a wage on which to live,
My precious time I have to give,
But one fine day I will retire,
And then fulfil my heart's desire,
To stop and rest, take time for me,
And visit those I seldom see.

M Wilcox

THE LEARNING JOURNEY

Learning is a journey with so many different routes,
A challenge, an adventure, which bears so many fruits,
It starts at realism, then moves along the path,
Passing through all doubts and fears, delights and aftermath,
One important question that the cross-roads will entail,
To take the straight and narrow road, or wander off and fail?
I watch out for the signposts, which tell me where to go,
Will I be successful, or left so full of woe?
There's one uncertain factor which lies beyond this bend,
But if we travel full of hope, success is at the end,
Perhaps we feel so negative, that we have failed somehow,
But if we've made our minds up and made one single vow,
To take advice from others will be one's utmost gain,
Well then, no matter what we think, our journey's not in vain.

Every day's a challenge, we must strive to reach our goal,
No one is too old to learn, each one can play their role,
From judges to a magistrate, from models to a star,
In working whilst still learning, there is nothing that can mar,
And when the days are captured in fog and pouring rain,
By improving with new knowledge, each day will be one's gain,
Some things will never happen, but how often we will try
To set tomorrow's pattern, and let the world go by.
How often we will panic, and dread the things to come,
Be worried or regretful of things we might have done,
Yet this may never happen, we have worried so in vain!
Why judge tomorrow's problems with the promise of more rain?
Learning is a journey, its successes can be measured,
And all the things that we've achieved are things that can be treasured.

Marjorie Picton

BEST THINGS IN LIFE

I couldn't be without you,
No matter where I roam,
Your smiles and chatter just
Brighten up my home.

My days you have filled with love,
I know you were all sent from
Heaven above.
Your photos sit upon my wall,
Your faces are a delight to see,
Especially when you smile,
As you sit upon my knee.

So innocent, so enquiring,
Wanting to learn,
Fun in the park, on the slides and swings,
On the beach, with the sand and shells,
Watching the seagulls on wing.

The Easter egg hunt was great fun,
As you giggled and shouted
Finding eggs for your tum.

The mess you made, the joy you gave
Is second to none,
From you, my lovely grandchildren.
You are growing up so quickly,
But my life without you would be empty.

Your hugs, cuddles, kisses and love,
I will hold in my heart, and hand,
Until I reach that promised land,
Thank you my lovely grandchildren . . .

Sylvia Kellett

WHO KNOWS HOW LONG!

Who knows how long we have on this planet of ours?
Years! Months! Days! Perhaps only hours!
We only get one chance at life, one time on Earth!
So just live life for all it's worth!

Given the chance we'll live for as long as we can!
Live it to the full, during our brief span.
Life is what you make it! So the experts say,
It's meant for living, each and every day!

To spend it with someone special, what more could we ask?
Would make it easier to face each daily task!
Just one more glance, a smile, one last kiss!
Makes life so worthwhile, not to be missed!

To spend life wisely, what more can we do?
Do it right, be happy, see it through!
Just one more day, perhaps an hour or two,
Time to spend with the one love for you!

Just one more look, one last embrace,
To see a smile upon your face!
To hold your hand, just one last touch,
Just one more time, would mean so much!

Our time on Earth, who knows how long?
Whatever life brings, just be strong!
With grim determination, see it through,
Forever thankful for time spent with you!

Richard Ninnis

THE BEST THINGS IN LIFE

The best things in life are free, or so they say.
The best things in life really are:
Good health, a happy home life
Happiness at work, a lovely home,
A welcoming family.

Trees and flowers, animals, the fish of the sea,
Sunshine and showers; and the moon and stars at night.
All are the best things in life.
The best thing in life - is also to
Live in a world where there is
Peace and plenty.

Janet Cavill

THE BEST THINGS IN LIFE

They say that the best things in life are free,
However, unfortunately, that does not include our TV,
Where would we be without our favourite soaps to watch every day,
From Coronation Street, EastEnders, Family Affairs to
Home And Away.
Sitting watching them each night with a cup of coffee in one hand,
As they sort out their daily lives and problems, making us understand,
We should be grateful for the little things we take for granted
and often ignore,
Like the wonders of nature around us and oh so much more.
A crisp, frosty, sunny morning when the sky is so clear and blue,
Do we ever really stop to be thankful and appreciate the view?
In the garden the many birds foraging for scraps of food,
making such a sound,
Bulbs starting to appear, their lovely bright colours soon
covering the dark ground.
A long walk through the fields, walking the dog, breathing in
such fresh air,
Perhaps we'll see a partridge she can chase, or better still a hare.
Coming home to listen to old Tamla Motown records and
reliving my past,
Recalling seeing some of the groups live, will these memories
forever last?

Dot Ridings

THE HUSH OF EVENING

Thank you for being you, dear friend
as I sit in the hush of the evening's glow,
the scent of memory settles on the wind
then light of those pleasant times does show.

Carefree and as the breezes in the trees
were those times when light of heart one loved,
then wished and hoped that time would freeze
the moment that one held in a hand, soft gloved,

That hush floating softly through one's life
to bring close to one's heart your touch,
thank you for entering into my life
to me your friendship does mean so much.

John Clarke

BEST THINGS IN LIFE

The best things in life really are free.
From the warm smile of a stranger on a frosty winter's day,
to the beautiful Turkish Delight hues of a sunset night.

Being gently woken by the sun's rays caressing your face.
Serenaded by the dawn chorus, how can you start the day
feeling glum?

Marvelling at the array of flowers in bloom.
Looking at the funny side of life without a care.
Feeling how lucky you are to be healthy and loved.
Appreciating each special moment in your life.
For me these things truly are the best things in life.

Candida Lovell-Smith

SEASONS OF LIFE

Childhood dreams are ones to treasure,
Just the kind which last forever.
They're of the season known as spring,
When we think we're sure of everything.

Life is harder when summer comes,
We have to work and do our sums.
Living the rat race is not much fun,
But alas, it has to be done.

When autumn comes we're often tired,
Perhaps! we think, we should retire.
After all, we've done our best
For others, and deserve a rest.

We soldier on through winter days,
It becomes a struggle in so many ways.
Stretching a pension isn't much fun,
But, somehow we manage and the battle is won.

Val Bermingham

GEMS FOR FREE

A shadow moon ghosts an ice crystal sky;
as a diamond solitaire sparkles the heavens,
gold cascades from the silver birth;
where rosehips gleam the hedgerows
in October's warm sunbeams,
a robin flashes his bright red breast,
his jet-black eyes twinkling.

Anita Richards

DISCOVERY

Do children still creep off in threes
To splash in streams, to climb up trees,
To cycle blind against the sun,
And roll down grassy banks for fun?

And do they trek out to the coast
And eat their lunch too soon, and boast
Of slaying dragons, winning wars,
And 'mine's a better dad than yours!'?

Do children still keep mice for pets,
And catch strange things in fishing nets,
And torment worms till kingdom come,
Pick dandelions for their mum?

If children don't still splash in streams,
And climb up trees, and dream their dreams,
And find fulfilment if they can,
What hope for Man?
What hope for Man?

Peter Davies

FOR ALL BUT THE BEST IS WITHIN

Life is but flavourless if only but flavourless
You make it
And less tasty begets
The more you neglect on to chew
Be the best thing in life unto those
Being how they escape it
And what manner of sensual purchase
They choose to renew

So filled be your host by emotions
Ethereal spirits at rest until drawn
Adventurers craving evocation
Remain until exorcised
Tethered unborn

Bring forth you that person
Within you resides
For 'tis life in itself that passes you by
Absorb you this gift by your seeing
Being a being of nature
Is by nature
The nature of being

All I could ever wish for
Are the things that I have today
Food and water
Shelter and sense
And a place for my dog to play

For by positive thought
Be all things the best things
So why don't you give it a try
Forget you that negative nemesis
And reach for the depths of the sky

Mark Anthony Noble

A PICTURE

(Day in the bog)

Every picture tells a story,
As does this - of nature's beauty.
Interrupted by Man's wholesome toil,
Reaping harvest from beneath the soil.

While dancing in the cool evening breeze,
Are the flossed cotton candy paws,
On this short mid-February day,
Surrounded by succulent marsh grasses at play.

A multiplex of gold and brown on green,
That engulfs the underfoot hidden bog.
While heralding in the coming spring,
With the reawakening wildlife song.

Mother Nature at her finest,
Shrouded in picturesque abundance.
Recolouring and regenerating each year,
Bringing forth a pleasant cheerful tear.

This story for me will always unfold,
Yet still be captured in painting bold.
Always there again to be retold,
Never being forgotten - or old.

Gary J Finlay

Best Things In Life

So many things in life to enjoy
From the simple, to the hard to explain
But for me, my family are a joy to behold
All the happiness, fun and the pain

From a single man to family of five
Two daughters, a son and a wife
The one I adore and a world full of love
And my future is set for life

First few years filled with strife
Just children, bringing up our young
But through all hard work and telling toils
Our children are a song to be sung

Pride in my family, love for them all
Fills my heart with a joy to behold
All my love and hopes for their lives
Keeps my heart warm, keeps out the cold

Family are a union, a solid embrace
A union that cannot be broke
My heart, my family, a solid base drawn
And a love I will never revoke

Richard Morris

ROCK-A-BYE BOATING

The pensioners' aid to rocking
Our men folk say in fun.
Then, putting on their sailors' hats
With engines set to run
We brave the angry river,
With chests held high and proud . . .
No fear or weakening quiver;
We smile at passing crowds.

Of course, I'm in the galley
Preparing heaps of food,
For later, down the valley . . .
We have to feed the brood.
The fishermen don't like us,
They frown as we go by;
They shake their heads, make such a fuss,
On that we can rely.

Our young ones lay about the decks
Enjoying nature's space,
Two fingers raised from land-bound necks
And words, not blessed in grace.
All sorts of people do it,
Some rich, and some quite poor.
We glide together through it.
As dancers glide the floor.

With old and young, plus middle aged,
As spring comes round once more . . .
We raise our glasses once again
And crave the boating shore.

Pearl M Burdock

HIGH DAYS AND HOLIDAYS

Lime the light,
some words of worth,
I'll bet this doesn't really work.
I'm trying to express in special ways,
those special times and halcyon days,
those high days and holidays.

When with the cars rolling on the roads,
the windows filled with regions slow
think of the old days, skies and suns,
the season's crazy gang, full of fun.

Pulling it to an olde worlde pub,
the talk like brass all in the smoke,
and ginger beer right over here,
brings back an age of innocence.

The children cried, and,
the world we live in caught the light -
we looked upon them all their lives,
we said goodbye to the seas at night -
shakes you're going to be something.

M C Jones

PRECIOUS DAUGHTERS

Like peas in a pod folk used to say
But they never seemed to me that way
Each one beguiling, smiling, different
One calm and serene, one always in a dream
The other smiling or laughing, a team
But all with their father's talents inherent

The eldest, his kindness and caring for others
She would see to her siblings and organise her mother's
terrible untidiness, forgetfulness too
She would clear up the kitchen and find that lost shoe

The next one, the dreamer, was helpful and good
And now she's achieved so much more than we could
She's tended the sick, the poor and the lame
And travelled abroad in Jesus' name

The youngest is bright and beautiful too
And uses her talents to help me and you
Just give her a challenge or a problem to solve
Oh darn it, I had better give this last line to her

The good thing about having a son is that he
chose a wife like a daughter to me
So now there are four lovely girls in our fold
Two grandkids and hubby and blessings untold

Barbara Harrison

SONGS WE SANG

A long time ago, thirty years or more
It could be longer, I'm not quite sure
Loitering around on corners we'd hang
So we formed a group called 'the bogie gang'.

We had a laugh, just harmless fun
But we'd always end up having to run
Scrumping apples nearly every day
Or knocking on doors and being chased away.

Riding our bikes or climbing walls
No broken bones but plenty of falls
Hopscotch, touch, postman's knock
Or playing war games around the block.

Visiting our dens in different places
Or dressing up and painting our faces
Carving our names into a tree
Or swinging on ropes for all to see.

We couldn't be still, we couldn't settle
We'd slide down fields on sheets of metal
Days on the beach, hours of fun
Tanning ourselves in the afternoon sun.

That was then, but this is now
Time's moved on, don't know how
Looking old, feeling young
Remembering happy songs we sung.

Brian Conway

THE SOUL'S PERSISTENT WHISPER

Little by little, bit by bit,
Cease all motion, just to sit.
Let the hum and drone go past,
Then the silence will be . . . at last.

The power of the silent time,
Is sent to teach us things sublime,
It shows us when and how and who,
The knowledge washes over you.

The ego hates the silent one,
So is full of evil fun,
The ego thinks the soul a fool,
Says I myself was born to rule.

But the soul can wait until end of time,
It's not deterred by ego shine,
When the ego ends its selfish blasts,
The soul's persistent whisper lasts.

Anthony Fagg

BLUEBELLS

I stand on the ridge
And overlook a field of bluebells
So blue it could be a lake

Bees buzz above the blossoms
Knocking into each other in mid-air
Whilst drinking their nectar

Beyond the bluebells a mountain range
White with snow caps touching the sky
White, sandwiched between the blues

And in the distance a goat-herd stands
Watching the goats frolic about
Their bells tinkling above the bluebells.

Jean Wallington

THE BESTEST IN ALL THE WORLD

Little Johnny says, 'My bestest thing in all the world is my
choo-choo train.'
'Roly-Poly Pudding is mine,' says Jane.
Adam admits he loves sucking his thumb.
Molly says it is Phillip, her baby brother,
But thinks that sometimes he's quite a bother.
'The bestest thing in all the world,' quotes Elsie, 'is my
dancing school.'
She cannot say if it is tap or ballet,
She just knows she loves her teacher, Mrs Ellee.
'My bestest thing in the entire world is my Lego,' says Jimmy,
'Or is it blancmange and jelly?'
'I love it when they are tucked up in bed at night,
To me it really is pure Heaven.'
These are the words of the mother of seven.

Elaine Priscilla Kilshaw

LITTLE WIGGLES
(Dedicated to Kurt John-Ray Summerfield)

I was told the pain would be forgotten,
as the pain was long, drawn-out,
I certainly hoped I would forget,
as the pain was excruciating beyond doubt.

I lay in shock at what was before me,
I was consumed with happiness that I began to cry,
and I hugged Gareth so tightly,
it was obvious our emotions were on a high.

As the days turned into months,
nature took its course,
and our son Kurt is growing ever so fast,
even at six months he has behind him a great force.

I love to look into his big blue eyes,
the eyes of his father,
just his smile brightens up my day,
I know no force could ever make my love waver.

I cannot help but stand by and watch him,
to witness his every move as he grows,
as he learns many things about the world,
but our true love for him I'm not sure he'll ever know.

Our love for him is *so* great,
no words I could use to describe,
as there are no words I could use,
but I know our love for him will *never* die.

He has many a nickname,
one is Kurtus-De-Borg which does make me giggle,
but the name which I believe describes him best,
would have to be the nickname 'Wiggles'.

Belinda Louise Summerfield

HEAVEN AND HELL

Mobile phones, cars and tube trains,
Knickers and pornography,
Socks with holes in, governments,
Chat rooms and advertisements.

Newspapers, tights and London,
Splinters and fortune-tellers,
Supermarkets, chemicals,
Schools and multinationals.

Lies and pain, death, disease.

My partner Nick, our flat,
Birds, gardens, dogs, our cat,
Earth, sun, mountains and sea,
Bats, pebbles, horses, tea,

Coffee, croissants, candle flames,
Bicycles on country lanes,
Books and music, foxes, grass,
Showers of rain quick to pass.

Moon and stars, flowers, trees.

E M Doyle

CARAVAN DAYS

This is my perfect place, my caravan park,
I wake to screeching gulls and the singing of larks,
There are footprints of rabbits on the soft sand outside,
The ocean thunders near at the turn of the tide,
Daffodils are dancing in the field over there,
Complete yellow carpets swaying in the air,
A footstep away the rocks call once more,
The sea has washed them and left seashells on the shore,
The surf is pure white as it crashes to the land,
When the wind whips the waves and patterns the sand,
Sun warms the small pools and we plodge with bare feet,
Fishing, running, playing makes our day complete,
We go searching for lobsters that are hidden in the bay,
Winkles too and crabs, these are glorious days,
All types of birds above us singing their songs,
Crickets click-clicking, summer days are so long,
A little mole lies lifeless on a grassy hill,
Shining black body, closed eyes and claws still,
All nocturnal creatures hide from the day,
From the brightness of sunshine and children at play,
Hedgehogs crawl slowly, searching for food,
And the woodpigeon hoots at the edge of the wood,
Red skies at evening glow with sunsets in the west,
Just leave me here, this is where I find rest,
This is my sanctuary from the mad dashing world,
Amongst all this splendour, it's my heaven unfurled.

Celia Auld

DREAMING

Best things in
Life are free,
As I sit in
The sun, knowing
That winter has
Come and gone,
Maybe a dip
In the sea,
While I dream
Away the day,
To read the poetry
Will bring it all
Real to me.
Happy days.

Barbara Brown

GRANDAD

I loved to visit Grandad, he was so old and grey,
He talked of long ago as if it were today.
When he was young, just like me, what he used to do,
Growing up, courting girls, I never dared ask who.

'Some day a lad will want you' he'd say and he would smile,
'You're going to be a little smasher, they will queue for miles'.
I'd blush, he'd hug me, he was so cuddly and kind,
He'd say how he met Gran, she was always on his mind.

'She's gone now lass, I miss her'. I could see his pain inside.
'Aye, she was such a bonny thing, lovely, sweet and kind,
What she saw in me? I don't know, perhaps it was my love,
That attracted her to me, or a message from above.

I met her at the dance', he'd said, 'at the local village hall,
First time I saw her, I asked could I come and call?
We'd hold hands, as we met, I tingled at her touch,
From then on, I fell for her, I loved her so much.

We married on the village gala day, there was such a crowd.
Her in her white wedding dress, my black suit, I was so proud.
Honeymoon in Scarboro', then back to our terraced home,
Young, naïve, so much in love, never more to roam'.

He had tears as he shrugged, 'Ah well, many years we had,
We had your mum, your auntie too, then you, we were so glad'.
He kissed me softly on the cheek, thanked me for visiting him,
In his little room, his TV, reading books, though his eyes were dim.

I never saw my grandad again, but he's so alive in me,
A character, always a tale to tell, with his mind so free,
He left a legacy of love, for Gran, and for us all,
I'll bet he's still spinning a yarn in some marbled hall.

George Carrick

TRUE LOVE

I love you just the same
As years ago when I took your name
In my heart and in my soul
Without you I'd feel not whole
Our hearts entwine, yours and mine
Bonded like a growing vine
As arms reach out for a warm embrace
We share a smile on our face
Nurture feelings deep inside
Our love too strong to hide
I look into your eyes so blue
Saying I love you too
I hear your laughter in my ear
Smell sweet aromas when you are near
My heart is pounding deep inside
A better love I will never find

Sheila Waller

A DAUGHTER'S THANK YOU

I'll always be there for you
Like all the times that you've been here for me too
Whenever I have needed to talk
Away, you were never the ones to walk

You have always been there for me
And you always see the best that there is to see
Supporting me in all my dreams
Never letting them fall apart at the seams

Because, for me you have always wanted happiness
And have always helped me to be my best
Whenever something happened that was bad
You somehow made me feel less sad

So thank you for the love you gave
Giving me the courage to be brave
Even though I sometimes made you mad
I just want to thank you for all the faith you had

Thank you for being who you are
Because that is what helped me get so far
And without you being here as I have grown
This happy life I would never have known.

Samantha Connolly

OUR MUM AND NAN

We never thought you'd leave us
We didn't think you'd go
We wonder if you realised how much we love you so
And even though you've left us
We know that you're still near
To help us and to guide us
And wipe away our tears
We think about you all the time
Each minute every day
We'll miss you for eternity
So what more can we say?
We know you're out there listening
And watching what we do
And so we're asking God above
To take great care of you

Sandra Jebb

GOD'S LITTLE ANGEL

I used to frequent this place,
My friend Larah's abode.
Her seven month old daughter, Thara
From birth with respiratory problems
Life hanging by the thread.
I visited one Friday
Watched angel Thara
Goo-gaaing and gurgling
Despite all her suffering.
Oh that mesmerising, enchanting smile
And an outpouring of love
She grabbed the tip of my index finger
In her small, soft, silky hand
Refusing to let go.
Then in a stroke and flash of lightning
Her smile in peace
She breathed no more
I, still in utter shock.

A Navamani

TO MY WONDERFUL GRAN . . . WITH LOVE
(Dedicated to Pam Webster)

When God invented grandmothers
He fulfilled all a child could ever need
And to have a gran like you
Is a very special blessing indeed!

From the very day I was born
Right through my life you've always been there
To love and cherish and nurture me
And to embalm me with your care.

You've acted as my guide
And taught me right from wrong
I couldn't have come this far
Without having had you beside me all along.

Even when the road's been rocky
You've helped to show me which path to choose
Gran, I know as long as I have you
I can never really lose!

For just the fact you're in my life
Is the greatest gift of all
To have you to encourage me -
To feel proud and to keep standing tall.

You really are one in a million
And I know I never could find
Someone quite as remarkable as you
For I do believe you're one of a kind.

I couldn't bear it should we ever be parted
For no one could ever take the place of you
I love you with all my heart Gran
With a love that's so grateful, so proud and will remain forever true!

Louise Pamela Webster

OUR DAUGHTER

Our daughter who we love so much,
Fills our lives with her love,
Will always be there,
And also show us lots of care,
She is funny and a joy to have,
She is intelligent,
Gentle and warm.

Our daughter,
She is a special person,
She will show her love,
In so many special ways,
She will always find time to help,
Those people that may ask,
Our daughter,
Who is a wonderful mother,
To our grandchildren.

Our daughter,
There is no other like you,
You will always be loved,
And will be our friend for life,
So to you our special daughter,
We give you all our love,
With all our heart,
Your loving parents,
May we never part.

Peter R Salter

GRUB UP

I wonder what has happened to,
The dishes of my youth,
The food I used to savour,
When I was younger in the tooth.
I never see a pan of scouse,
Or a plate of tripe and onion,
'Get it down, it's good for you'
Was Mother's firm opinion.
I could enjoy a dripping butty,
A lot tastier than jam,
During rationed war years,
Civvies had dried eggs and Spam.
Somehow Mother managed,
Without microwave or freezers,
How would she have catered,
With beefburgers, yoghurts and pizzas.

Brian O'Brien

BRANCHING OUT

Memories of childhood days we share
When all the family was still there

There were four sisters including me
Also three brothers make the family tree

But one sister has passed away
And still we grieve every day

Our lovely mum is no longer here
How we love and miss her dear

But through the sun's golden rays
We recall the past of bygone days

Those happy days when we were together
Will be with us forever and ever

The main branch of our home has now gone
Still her perfume of life lingers on

It's not for us to sit and weep
Instead tears of laughter upon our cheeks

We keep remembering those happy times
Yes of course we do, but then there's sighs

Josephine Anne Dunworth

MY WIFE, MY LIFE

In the distance I saw you wearing that yellow dress
I didn't know you then; you belonged to another, nevertheless
You had just turned the corner, blonde hair back-lit by the sun
We started to talk, you were after some fun.

You are someone so special, a little gem
That very rare person who appears now and then.

We met every Tuesday in a secret place
Such a classy lady with a beautiful face
So comfortable to be with, it was easy to talk
We had to be careful in case we were caught.

My first thought when I wake, my last when I sleep
The first I tell of good news, the first when I feel weak.

Then he was gone, together at last
I met with your children, were we going too fast?
When I moved in I brought you a ring
I could only hope we were doing the right thing.

You touch the lives of all that you know
You're the only one that can't see it though.

Now as my wife you are unsurpassed
The years have gone by all too fast
Money was short, we overcame many fears
Supporting the children in their difficult years.

Your devotion to your family with your unconditional love
The love for your animals is second to none.

Eighteen years later I love you so much
With your caring nature and gentle touch
You always said our meeting was fate
Now we are each other's soulmates.

Philip Peartree

MY FATHER

My father was my heart's delight,
He made my day,
He put his arms around me,
And showed me the way.
He bathed me, he washed me,
He brushed my hair,
He gave me a life,
Without any care.
We laughed, we smiled through the day,
And he was the one who taught me to say,
'I love you'.
We fed the rabbits, we fed the hens,
Cleaned out the hutches, and the pens,
Watered the flowers day by day,
Wrapped the eggs in buckets of hay,
And there is to him one thing I must say,
'I love you'.

Ann Margaret Rowell

LUNA

Long brown curls glint auburn in the sun
Streaming in through clear glass
This cold December day
Capturing a moment I'd never known before
Until seeing this sleek, equine-bodied soul
Exuding innocence
And standing there, open-mouthed and gazing
With a doleful stare
Her laughing fingers brush all doubt away
And start the axis spinning

Desmond Swords

THANK YOU

Having appreciation comes through communication
It gives determination when you spread your appreciation
So don't give up, the temptation shows lots of appreciation
And you will create love and determination.

M Smith

SOMEONE I NEVER KNEW

I didn't see the child at play
Or the roguish boy at school
The choirboy bent on knee to pray
The youth who broke the rule
I didn't see the gymnast leap
Or the soldier leave the plane
The hero or the husband
'Twas all before I came
I didn't see you as you grew
From life the page was torn
I saw a father's eyes of blue
Look down when I was born.

Susan Fear

WITH YOU
(Dedicated to Wim Faassen. See, I did get you a present)

With you came sorrow, pain.
With you came tearstained pillows.
With you came grief and sleepless nights.
With you came sickness, fright.
With you came fear and nightmares.
With you came a sadness unquenchable.
With you came regret, bitter and terrible.
With you came thoughts of death.
With you came truth, harsh and cruel.
With you came never-ending torment.
With you came loneliness unbearable.

But as time drew on, a shadow lifted,
I was blessed, my perspective shifted.

With you came laughter, joy.
With you came tears of triumph.
With you came a happiness with no match.
With you came dreams that I could catch.
With you came stability.
With you came companionship and loyalty.
With you came a light to bring the day.
With you came a map to find the way.
With you came guidance, a role model.
With you came ideas, bright and resourceful.
With you came love.

Tiffany Little

AUNT EDITH'S BIRTHDAY TREAT

Her hooded eyes, her creased throat,
Gravelled, husky tones,
A straight-backed, hands crossed pose,
And catalogue of moans.

We shared birthdays in July,
But seventy years apart.
With cemetery tread she came to cast
Her shadow on my heart.

Black shoes, black bag, her mourning best
A dark funeral gloss,
She'd lift her veil and then begin
Her liturgy of loss.

Who had died of what last week,
Whose funeral went well,
Those clinging on, but destined
Soon to hear the bell.

She pulled me closer, to her
Dry doom-laden breath.
My child's lips touched her withered cheek,
My yearly brush with death.

J Dalton Taylor

TOGETHER WE . . .

Together we zigged and zagged so stealthily,
albeit somewhat unhealthily
through Richmond park's deer-dungy grass of which we pass -
not pardon.
Together we niggled and nagged so hilariously;
so be it, somewhat precariously
stoop at riverside, from which we espied at little minnow's garden.

Together we're rest-assured at the behest of nevertheless,
spring's wind-test
of river distended; shivering in its winnowing of our quivering
words to render unintended edit.
Together we're nest-inured, as in the minnow's domain,
nonetheless, to witness the contended grain-rain until summer's
coming still did tender intended remit.

Together we were without cutlery or plate and so ate whatever -
unlike the minnow's hasty forays to evade peckish pike - however we
chose today's friendship as our tasty, fresh rosebud.
Together we were without butlery or wait and no negate
whatsoever; thus without cuss did consummate
our repose whenever, with keener teeth - not nose
for pungent heath by 'chewing the cud'.

Together we thought that we ought
not to think therefore as guest or host, inasmuch as there need be to
drink a toast to the health - as in amenity - to the wherefore wealth
of nature's passage rites.
Together we in cohort with fishes consort
not to be lured into our niches as such,
just inured to the rough and smooth of life's bitches and riches,
we groove out our ways by sharing sun rays and bearing insect bites.

Gerald Weeks

SISTERS

As I look back on our childhood
with fond memories
I smile to myself and chuckle with glee
at all the good times we had.
We played, we fell out like all children do.
Sisters we are in good times and bad.
As we grow older and wiser with years
we have our families with our own ideas
but listen to this and listen well
if I could choose sisters I'd choose you again
because you are my friend as well as my sister.

Lorraine Booth

5 YEARS AGO

5 years ago today
You left my life
No coming back
No time left on this Earth.

5 years ago today
You left my life
And you didn't say goodbye
You left me all alone.

5 years ago today
You left my life
Why did you do that to me?
I can't just let you go
I just can't move on.

Nikki Rogers

PRECIOUS MOMENTS
(A special birthday)

Precious moments together we shared,
With family and friends who really cared,

Magic moments of time which has gone,
Memories that can lift you up and linger on,
With favourite pictures, music and song,

Precious moments for all of us to share,
If we look all around us they are everywhere.

David Wright

FAREWELL

We gathered for her final day
Aware of vanished years
Remembering the things she said
Holding back our tears

Planned for almost twenty years
She chose the hymns we sang that day
Even in death her presence felt
She had the final say

The eulogy described her life
Independent, ever proud
Never afraid to speak her mind
She stood out from the crowd

A simple life of ordinariness
Based on family, cats and home
For over sixty years she cared for them
Nearly thirty on her own

Failing sight made each day harder
Arthritis brought more pain
The outside toilet off the yard
Checked each and every day

Her final years were easier
Although the home was sold
To help meet the nursing costs
The price of growing old

A sad reflection on our time
When such independence goes
To see the many grasping benefits
She decided to forego

Despite these thoughts, memories remain
Of a life that used to be
The love and comfort over years
Particularly for me.

Martin Blakemore Davis

TORN

Problems are burying me, thick and fast,
I thought it would be alright, I knew it wouldn't last.

Cried so hard, can't cry any more,
Tired, exhausted, my eyes are so sore.

Being tortured and tormented by a weakness you've found,
My world's been shattered, been turned upside down.

I hear the shouts and the blames,
Everything I'm used to has gone up in flames.

Once was solid as a rock, we stick together through thick and thin,
Was once as a unit, no one could get in.

We love each other and really care,
Someone would knock us, no one would dare.

You'd hurt the one and you'd get us all,
Kick one of us and we would all fall.

Hearing others cry, that hurts the most,
You see everyone happy, look at them boast.

If I'm unhappy you should be too,
Why did this happen to me and not you?

Looking at me, 'Well, what are you looking at?'
Asking, 'Are you okay?'
'I'm fine!' I spat.

'Well, are you okay? Are you alright?'
I won't sit and cry, I won't go down without a fight.

You have to be the strong one and pull everyone through,
I can't do this alone, I'm human like you.

Friends coming up to me, saying, 'I've been through it too.'
Well you don't know how I feel, it's different for each and
                                    every one of you.

You don't know how I feel, you can't comprehend,
It feels so different, it feels like the end.

Please don't leave me, I need you all,
We're weak as individuals, but strong as a whole.

Everything's different, start new, start fresh,
Maybe I don't want that . . . well couldn't you have guessed?

Melanie May

THE MIRROR

Wave to a friend in the mirror,
a stranger, not me at all.
A woman with a warm smile is
holding him, she is full of grace,
yes I know her face.

Flame-red spiky hair
and a million freckles
that go everywhere.
'Hello to me.'
Big strong arms
are holding me up
so that I can see
this is my daddy.

Standing on 'tippy-toes'.
I can see my face up
to my nose.
If I stand even taller,
stick out my tongue
and lean really close,
that's great, I look gross!
'If the wind turns,
your face will stay like that!'
Grandma declares whilst fixing
her hat.

What's more like Hell, freckles or spots?
I wish I could swap the lot,
for something better,
don't know what.

'Will you marry me?' is that okay?'
If I practice any longer
I'll be here all day.

'Hello reflection, it's me again.'
Through sadness and happiness
we've come a long way.

When I'm gone from this place,
I promise to visit,
to me you are eternally exquisite!

Kay Hancock

A BEAR AND TWO MINTS

Each morning he'd welcome us
into the vapour of his Oxford-twilled legs,
lining up Christine, Penelope, and a bear called Keith,
in descending order of height,
along the back of his
bed-settee.

Two extra strong mints would be
enthroned upon each knee,
the holes in their centres - like specks on a shelf -
winking at me and sis.

At lunch time he'd lure us back,
the sea-smog of his stout slithering down
inside its polished glass and with tell-tale
interpretations tempt us aground.

'I killed a Zulu once,' he drawled.

Ready for bed and trumped up on my father's shoulders,
I saw the old man through a crack of our customary closed front door,
willing them to turn his room the right way round,
him sickening with its motion as his right side withered.

That next day, trundling toys out into the sun,
I could hear him still,
shouting for his black, black Mary.
It was then that I learnt to join up he's gone, he's gone, he's gone
with tears of prostrate women.

AnnMarie Eldon

My Family

If I had my life to live over again
Not a single thing would I ever change
I've had my sorrows and happiness too
Some days have been happy and others blue
But compared to some I'm rich by far
With a wonderful husband I feel like a star
And my wonderful children, not perfect it's true
But they are my life I must tell you
No matter what comes I will always cope
As each day I live I know there's hope
So I pray in the future I'm not left alone
After all of this happiness I have known.

Sylvia J Barbier

FIERY INFLUENCE!

A little boy, a young boy
once met the little people
out there in the wood - simply
on his own - beyond the stars,
in a cold and lonely night
in the night of the beast,
once: when lycanthropy nightmares
dance through children's heads,
and they pray to God they'll
fall asleep and awake alive
in their beds to see the sun.
So lost, confused, scared,
he wants to run away until
the moon and stars light up
the night: the beast
will soon be here.
Silence crashes down like
a sharp knife, a sound
cuts it through.
The beast is coming . . .

The moon still shines, but not
as brightly, and not for long.
Darkness prophetic of evil.
Even the little owl doesn't
call; everything bodes
ill. The boy is
so scared, yet he doesn't
give a bucket of tears
as others might! He is brave!

Though the beast makes his blood
run cold. He shivers, and kneels.
His prayer sends a sign
to the little people with their fairy lights.
Oh, a fire sign! A candle in the dark!
Fiery influence!

George Penev

JOAN

I love to sit and talk to you
About days of yesteryear,
How we laughed and giggled
Without a single care.
Winter saw us playing
In the snow and in the sleet,
Wearing socks upon our hands
As well as on our feet.
Leather boots, what were they?
Not for the likes of us,
Wellingtons chaffed our legs
But we never made a fuss.
We would walk along the river Cole
Run in and out the trees,
Always going home
With scratched and bloody knees.
Cycling to the bluebell woods
On bikes made out of scrap,
We'd pick some flowers for Mother
Then happily peddle back.
I never see a fresh mown field
Or wildflowers in all their hue,
Unless my mind goes racing back
To childhood days I spent with you.

Dot Brown

ADVICE TO A SON

More the fool to follow a cad,
When senses lack direction,
Please listen to me now, my lad,
It's time for life's correction.

Ill-gotten gains show no reward,
A more civil life is essential,
The conscience clear sleeps at night,
A troubled mind is mental!

Fill the missing gaps in life,
Confidence can be restored for a winner,
Use God's gift to fight the strife,
More the fool to be a sinner.

My son, my son, what can I say,
But pray indeed you will listen,
And come back from where you strayed,
To begin another mission.

Where is your sense of goodness,
The innocence you portrayed in youth?
You follow now a trail of foolishness,
You bounder to be uncouth.

Oh, my lad, what can one do,
But tell you wrong from right,
And pray that God will help you,
In achieving good insight.

William Archibald

JUST SAY NO

I have two sons called Dean and Wayne
Without them life wouldn't be the same
They help me keep my life on track
I'm nearly clean and not looking back

I see them mostly at weekends
The love they give my life depends
They mean the world and more to me
I'm really proud of my family tree

I always ring and then they call
And when we meet we have a ball
I explained to them I used to use
The ups and downs and moody blues

So if you're offered when in school
Just say, 'No, I'm not a fool'
Walk away and have no fear
Your life you'll have and a good career

Tim Thompson

MEMORIES

(For my mother-in-law)

I only have to close my eyes
And think of times gone by
And all the things you taught me
I see in my mind's eye
From cooking, sewing and being a mam
You taught me many things
Just thinking of the good times
And my heart sings
The day we went to Cleethorpes
And you tried to pour the tea
The bus was bumping badly
And you spilt it on your knee
Your grandchildren still love you
And laugh about that day
And wish with all their hearts
That the Lord had let you stay
The memories we cherish
And the love you gave to all
The way you handled ups and downs
And always had a smile
We miss you Mam and always will
Because we love you so
But memories keep us going
And they always will.

Hilda Morrall

TO RITA

My shoulder in the darkest times;
companion in the good.
You've been my friend these many years,
and many tears withstood.

To have you as my confidante;
to answer each request;
to have a friend like you
I know I'm truly, truly blessed.

Your soul is born from up above.
Your goodness shining strong.
Your wisdom knows no boundaries.
Your judgement never wrong.

Your patience never ending.
Your compassion real and true.
Your thoughtfulness for others
in the things you say and do.

Each life you touch is gratified.
Each hand you hold is graced.
Each soul you share your caring with
feels warmed by your embrace.

You've had your many troubles;
a bigger share than most;
and yet you find the strength
to cope with all that you have lost.

You are the 'special lady', if ever one there was.
Experiences teach us all what matters most to us.

Sometimes I feel unworthy to have you as my friend,
as I could ne'er repay you in a lifetime without end.

But know this now and always, from the bottom of my heart,
there's not another living soul could ever take your part.

Shirley Ann Bunyan

To My Friend

Did I tell you
how much I love
the way you hug me,
the way you flash your smile
up at me, its dimpled corners
reflecting rays of hope
even when the clouds are low?
The way you let me be me,
and let me be someone else;
not judging either
just accepting who they are.
But most of all I love
how you make everything
better than it should be.

Peter Holmes

SUBMISSIONS INVITED
SOMETHING FOR EVERYONE

OVER £10,000 POETRY PRIZES TO BE WON!

POETRY NOW 2004 - Any subject,
any style, any time.

WOMENSWORDS 2004 - Strictly women,
have your say the female way!

STRONGWORDS 2004 - Warning!
Opinionated and have strong views.
(Not for the faint-hearted)

All poems no longer than 30 lines.
Always welcome! No fee!
Cash Prizes to be won!

Mark your envelope (eg *Poetry Now*) **2004**
Send to:
Forward Press Ltd
Remus House, Coltsfoot Drive,
Peterborough, PE2 9JX
(01733) 898101

If you would like to order further copies of this
book or any of our other titles, please give us a
call or log onto our website at
www.forwardpress.co.uk